Self Defence in Action

Robert Clark

Stanley Paul
London Melbourne Auckland Johannesburg

Stanley Paul & Co. Ltd

An imprint of Century Hutchinson Ltd
62–65 Chandos Place, London WC2N 4NW

Century Hutchinson Australia (Pty) Ltd
PO Box 496, 16–22 Church Street, Hawthorn,
Melbourne, Victoria 3122

Century Hutchinson New Zealand Limited
PO Box 40–086, Glenfield, Auckland 10

Century Hutchinson South Africa (Pty) Ltd
PO Box 337, Bergvlei 2012, South Africa

First published 1987

© Robert Clark 1987

Set in Monophoto Times

Printed in Great Britain by Butler & Tanner Ltd
Frome and London

British Library Cataloguing in Publication Data
Clark, Robert
    Self defence in action.
    1. Self-defense
    I. Title
    6134.6′6   GV1111

ISBN 0 09 166371 7

Contents

Acknowledgements

I would like to express my appreciation of the role played in the production of this book by David Mitchell of the Martial Arts Commission.

I am also grateful to my students who willingly provided their time and efforts to be photographed in this book, and to Roy Pell for the sequence photographs.

Introduction

There is more rubbish talked about self defence than anything else to do with the martial arts. People study the martial arts and assume this automatically qualifies them in self defence; but it does not.

The martial arts were originally formulated to provide soldiers with a collection of techniques they could use on the battlefield. As military techniques changed, so some arts became obsolete whilst others changed. Those which became obsolete were sometimes retained as a form of mental training, or changed into a combat sport. Some techniques were altered; others were left out altogether. The object was now to win points or to achieve inner calm.

Not all martial arts underwent this change. My own art, jiu jitsu, is one of the oldest practised, yet it has not become obsolete. Jiu jitsu contains traditional practice forms which used to protect the ancient Samurai warrior. It also contains modern police self-defence techniques, which teach us how to counter threats from modern weapons such as a firearm.

Jiu jitsu-based self defence has never relied upon an 'all or nothing' response

common to those martial arts devised around striking systems. For this reason it remains more suitable to professions such as the police, where self defence has to take into account a public acceptability factor. The concept of a police officer kicking or punching a member of the public is unacceptable, and this is why jiu jitsu provides the ideal answer.

I have travelled the world and studied with the masters of many other disciplines, and wherever I saw a good technique or a useful system I have incorporated it into jiu jitsu. My yardstick has been simply one of effectiveness. It is this willingness to evolve that has made jiu jitsu into the most suitable self-defence system for today's needs.

Despite this continual evolution, jiu jitsu has remained true to the original concept of using an opponent's force to his own disadvantage. If you match strength with strength, you will lose to the stronger person, but if you use his strength against him, then no matter how strong he is, or even how weak you are, he can never defeat you.

Let me give you an example. If someone pushes me, I don't fight back against that push. I harmonize with it, pulling my opponent off balance. Of course it is never as easy as that, and sometimes a little diversion such as a sharp blow to the opponent's ribs is necessary to create an opening.

When I make that blow, I use neither tremendous power nor strength; I apply just enough force to a vulnerable part of my opponent's anatomy to provide sufficient time for a secondary technique.

This use of resilience rather than confrontation is the hallmark of jiu jitsu, the 'Compliant Way'.

Having excellent techniques is only a part of effective self defence. The most effective techniques count for nothing if you can't bring yourself to apply them under pressure. Therefore training methods must be based on realism.

I never permit single-sex classes, because this prevents a woman from learning how to cope with the sheer size and strength of a man. I insist that powerful, realistic attacks are made, with no concession to smaller or weaker students. A student who learns how to defend against weak or unfocused attacks will be ineffective against the real thing.

Hard training furnishes another benefit. It cultivates in the student the desire to succeed, the will to win. There is no better self defence than the absolute refusal to lose. This has nothing at all to do with physical size or strength; it is purely mental. Of course vigorous training does discourage many students, but such people would never be able to learn truly effective self defence. The student who trains hard and completes

9

the course must be careful to avoid over-confidence. Complacency is a dangerous obstruction to good self defence.

I cannot hope to show here the full scope of my martial art, but I will try to whet your appetite.

Like all things learned for the first time, they will require a great amount of initial effort before their performance becomes second nature and can be performed without conscious thought. When you are attacked, you simply won't have time to think about which move follows what.

When you begin, your partner must cooperate to make it easy for you to apply the technique you wish to practise. Later, when you have learned how to apply it properly, make your partner attack really hard. Realism during training is the cornerstone of effective practice.

I recommend that you join a club where effective self defence is taught. Under the watchful eye of a capable coach your mistakes will be more quickly seen and remedied, and you will become competent in a shorter space of time.

Robert Clark
National Coach,
British Jiu Jitsu Association
Liverpool, September 1986

Stand up for yourself

It is a sad fact that the weak are natural targets for the aggressor. The quiet and nervous person stands a greater chance of attack than the assertive individual. What is the difference between the two?

Body language and perhaps the pheromones indicate a potential victim. I am not a psychologist but I have no difficulty in telling if someone is ill at ease or nervous. Their refusal to lock gazes and the way they stand, with hunched shoulders and lowered eyes, mark them as a potential victim. Confronted by a dominant individual, they seemingly shrink in upon themselves, passively accepting domination.

Stand straight and look directly into the other person's eyes. If the person threatening you is standing, then you must stand also. Relax your shoulders and hold your head up. Let your arms hang naturally at the sides of your body. Stand at a slight angle to the other person but turn your head to keep him fully in sight. Slow your breathing and try not to tense.

Keep your features relaxed and as emotionless as you can manage. Don't smile or look wildly about. Stare the person in the eyes and hold his gaze. Do not break your gaze to look down.

The frightened person's voice is querulous or hesitant. Don't bluster or repeat yourself but speak firmly in a normal tone of voice. Do not chatter and respond only when necessary, restricting your answer to the minimum of words. False bravado is easily detected because the words used do not match the body language. Try and take the heat out of the situation by not responding to insults or threats.

You don't have to be big to be good at self defence. It helps if you are but, believe me, a physique like a weightlifter is no substitute for an indomitable will. I know several small people that could never be targets for attack, because they are obviously strong individuals. Conversely, I know some big people who are basically weak and, despite their size, make high-profile targets.

Don't let yourself be dominated.

Take precautions

Only a fool goes blindly into a potentially dangerous situation. You feel a hand on your shoulder and what do you do? Do you just look round anyway and perhaps get the business end of a pint glass in your face? Or do you glance down at the attacker's fingers and check which side the thumb is on? Knowing which hand is touching your shoulder tells you which way to turn and what precautions are needed. Turn in the wrong manner and you could directly face his other hand and whatever it might be holding. The reflection in a mirror or shop window can help you assess what's going on behind you.

Observation helps you avoid areas of potential danger, and you should try to set up a system where simple commonsense precautions operate without conscious thought. The following are some elementary safeguards:

Don't sit with your back to a door but arrange yourself instead so you can see the room. If possible, sit between a table and the wall. Check the room for exits and obstructions.

Keep the doors to your house locked, especially at night, and install and use a porch light. If you have a security chain, make sure it is screwed securely into stout wood and can withstand a hefty impact from boot or shoulder. If you

13

aren't expecting callers, do not open the door without first checking identities through a door viewer. Do not allow two or more strangers to enter under any circumstances.

Sit near the driver when you travel by bus. On a train, choose a carriage where there are lots of people and if they all get out at a station, get out too and look for another carriage.

When driving, lock your car doors and do not pick up hitchhikers. If you are faced with attack whilst in the car, keep sounding your horn until help appears.

Do not pull up next to a fight that is in progress. If you feel you can render positive assistance other than simply by calling the police, then park a distance up the road and walk back. Don't intervene in an evenly matched fight because both parties may decide to have a go at you instead. If you must do something, wait until one of the combatants is clearly getting the worst of it so at least he will applaud your action. It takes at least two people and preferably more to effectively separate and keep apart a pair of fighters.

If someone threatens you, do not make an inflammatory response. Try to walk away and do not respond to provocation or insult. Always keep cool and reason with the person.

Avoid overt signs of anxiety, since these inflame certain types of potential attacker. If someone believes you have offended them, offer apologies, even when you have nothing to apologize for.

A practical response should be used only as a last resort

15

How hard can I respond to an attack?

This is a good question. There are cases when a victim responds to attack with such violence that he, rather than the attacker, has been prosecuted. A self-defence situation can be extremely frightening and you may react with panic, but the court which later examines the outcome does so dispassionately, and what seemed appropriate at the time can later appear as over-reaction.

You must therefore quickly assess the potential level of personal danger facing you. Is this a spontaneous argument between two adults over some slight? Or is it a predetermined attack in which the intent is obviously to cause you serious injury? Is there more than one attacker? Are weapons visible?

All these are factors to take into account when assessing the degree of personal danger. The greater danger you believe you are facing, the more force you can use in your own defence.

If more than one person attacks you, or you are menaced with weapons, then you may have grounds for arming yourself. Your intent in all cases must be simply to escape injury, using as little

16

force as is possible to accomplish this. If you succeed in defeating the attacker, do not then stoop to additional and unnecessary acts of violence against him.

The techniques contained in this book can be performed in such a way as to control the degree of pain inflicted. I have avoided techniques which are highly damaging to the attacker. By application of these selected techniques to the necessary degree (and no more), you will be making a reasonable response to any attack.

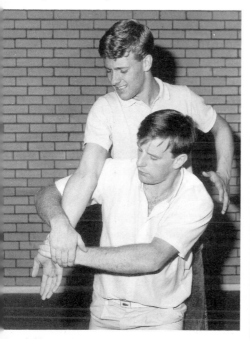

Inflict pain without causing unnecessary injury

17

Weapons in self defence

Bearing in mind the caution expressed in the previous chapter, the victim may try to use a weapon for defensive purposes. However, unless you are prepared to use it and know how to, it is best not to take it up. A weapon can be taken away and used against you, so don't bluff. If you are not prepared to use a weapon, don't pick one up.

A brandished weapon must have deterrent value. It must appear clearly of itself to be capable of inflicting injury. A carving knife is better in this respect than a rolling pin. The weapon must be suitable for use within the attack situation. For example, it is difficult to use an umbrella in a telephone box.

If the weapon is to be used as a frightener, then jab it at the attacker's face with short moves that pull it away quickly from grasping hands. Long curving slashes are easily countered and will result in the weapon being taken away. If the weapon is not to be used as a deterrent, keep it concealed until needed.

The object of using a weapon should not be to kill the attacker, but rather to cause such pain that he becomes dissuaded from pursuing the attack. There-

18

fore use the weapon on vulnerable but not fatal targets such as the arms and legs, aiming for the well-muscled areas. Stay away from the stomach, chest, neck or face.

Don't swing a baton because the heavier it is, the slower it is, and the more easily avoided. Jab at the groin or face with it and, if you get the chance, club at the base of the neck, the elbows, or the knees.

Flour, sand, or even soil can be flung into the attacker's face. This will buy valuable seconds during which time you can make your escape. Chairs and tables can be upended in the path of an attacker and anything heavy that comes to hand can be thrown.

A weapon must come easily to hand. Don't waste time fumbling in drawers; use this time instead to escape.

19

A place to train

The techniques shown in this book can be practised in any area where there is enough space to move around. Don't practise on a hard floor, because the throws involve landing with a fair amount of force, and it takes skill to land safely on a hard surface.

Judo mats are best, but agility mats will do as long as they don't slide apart. Don't train near tables, chairs, wallbars or anything you can bash into. Keep well away from glass doors and low windows and make sure there are no low light fittings. Open a window or two for a good through-flow of ventilation.

Wear old clothes you don't mind getting torn. I don't recommend training in free-fitting leisure wear or specialist martial art tunics, because they provide a freedom of movement you won't experience with street clothes. Wear trainers or go barefoot but, if the latter, have your partner go barefoot too. Don't wear spectacles because they are all too easily broken. Be careful with contact lenses – in the hurly-burly of training, they are frequently lost.

Necklaces can cause painful injuries to the neck and throat if worn during training. Metal hair grips, rings, watches and earrings can also be dangerous. If

20

you can't get your ring off, tape it over. Keep long hair tied back with elastic bands and ensure that your fingernails are clean and cut short. Since training brings you into close contact with other people, make sure your standard of personal hygiene is adequate.

It is better to train in a club than at home. Few of us can sustain the motivation to train hard when there is no-one pushing us. A club provides an opportunity to train with different people; it also provides you with expert supervision so that your mistakes can be detected and rectified at an early stage.

If you do decide to train at a club, pick one that is recognized by the Martial Arts Commission. It doesn't matter what certificates the instructor shows you – the only one that matters is the MAC Coach Certificate, which identifies a safe and competent teacher. There is no substitute for Martial Arts Commission recognition.

The Martial Arts Commission, or 'MAC' as it is usually called, was set up in 1977 by the heads of Britain's martial art governing bodies. The British Jiu Jitsu Association was a founder member. We recognized a need to agree standards of practice, which would both maintain high levels of proficiency and make the martial arts safer for the general public.

There is a minority of martial arts groups that are not part of the Com-

mission. These are associations which will not accept our control, or which are not sufficiently competent to be admitted into membership.

There is just one form of licence issued to all practitioners of the martial arts, regardless of whether they train in jiu jitsu, kung fu, or whatever. The Martial Arts Commission Licence is issued to all participants in the martial arts, teachers and students alike. It includes a valuable insurance policy which not only indemnifies you against injuring your partner but also provides a personal accident cover.

The Martial Arts Commission is the only body to operate a proper coaching scheme to make sure you are taught good technique in a safe way. It is also the only organization to require that all its coaches hold professional indemnity insurance.

The Martial Arts Commission Licence is issued through the British Jiu Jitsu Association and, if you have any enquiries about joining, please contact the Martial Arts Commission, 15/16 Deptford Broadway, London SE8 4PE, or the British Jiu Jitsu Association, WJJF, Barlows Lane, Fazakerly, Liverpool L9 9EH.

Fit to train

The self-defence student must obviously be fit enough to withstand the demands of training. If you are so puffed you have difficulty keeping up with the class, then you will not be able to concentrate on getting your techniques correct.

The fitness requirement for the course is not very high and should not disqualify anyone of any age from participating. Fitness is not the product of regular exercising alone, it is the outcome of a healthy way of life. Improve your health by correct nutrition. Eat regular small meals and go easy on animal protein. Reduce your fat and sugar intake as much as possible and increase the number of vegetables you eat. Do not smoke.

People with health conditions likely to affect their training should consult a doctor after first looking at the training.

Never train on a full stomach, otherwise you may experience cramp. Neither should you train during bouts of 'flu because certain strains of virus can irritate the heart. If you suffer from asthma, keep your inhaler at hand. Diabetics must have a handy source of sugar nearby. Even when you are fully fit, do not train too hard. Train within your own limits and stop when a breather is necessary.

Unless you are a manual worker, your muscles will be unequal to the demands of training, so loosen up before training. Run on the spot, raising your knees and arms as high as possible. Alternatively jump up and down on the spot, taking an extra high leap and tucking your feet up every tenth jump.

Press-ups are good for strengthening chest muscles, but practise them properly by keeping your back straight throughout and looking forwards instead of at the floor. Sit-ups will tone stomach muscles but keep your legs bent at all times or you will injure your back.

When you feel warm enough, do some gentle stretching exercises that loosen your joints. Move them through their full range in a smooth, non-stressful manner. Don't fling your arms and legs about.

Stretch muscles by taking them to their maximum length. While holding the stretch, try and contract them, then relax to get a couple of extra inches of movement. Hold the greatest stretch you can manage for a count of ten.

Only practise exercises which are non-injurious. Avoid those which put excessive stress on the musculo-skeletal system. Don't bounce on stretched limbs and avoid sudden excessive pressure applied by enthusiastic exercise partners.

Try to keep active and warm during training and sit out of cold draughts. At the end of your lesson, do a graduated

24

series of exercises to return you to a normal state of muscle function. These will be similar to those of the loosen-up, but this time the purpose is to pump the fluid which has accumulated during training out of the muscles. If this is not done, stiffness and soreness will result.

Flexible joints are invaluable in this kind of training!

25

Falling correctly

During practice you are going to end up on the floor, so begin training by learning how to land safely. On the street where there are no mats to protect you, knowing how to fall correctly is a vital element of self defence. You must be able to land safely from any position when tripped or thrown.

The forward roll-out is the best to start with. Bend forwards from the waist and put the palm of your right hand on the floor just in front of your left foot. Bend your elbow slightly and tuck your head in as you roll forward along the curve of your arm. Gather your feet in as you finish rolling and stand up quickly.

The forward roll translates the vertical movement of a fall into a horizontal one. The body must be relaxed during the roll. Drunkards often fall from great heights without injuring themselves, because they are totally relaxed.

When you feel confident at doing the forward roll-out, try going faster into it. Jump high into the air as you lead-in.

Next try a backward roll-out, using your arms to slap down on the mat. Get into a crouching position and tuck your head onto your chest. Roll onto your back and slap down with both arms to break the fall. Keep your arms straight and strike the mats with your palms. Do not let your elbows hit the mat first.

When you feel more confident, begin from a standing position but be sure to sit down as you fall back. Keep your chin pressed against your chest throughout.

To practise side breakfall for the first time, lie on the mat and roll from side to side. As you do so, slap the mat with each arm alternately. When you feel confident, go to a squat and deliberately unbalance yourself by lifting one leg clear of the ground and swinging it across in front of the other. Do this on both sides. Eventually you will be able to start from a standing posture. Kick across the front of one leg with the other, throwing yourself off balance and to the side. Try to land hip first in a rolling motion and slap palm downwards with a straight arm. Practise side breakfall on both sides.

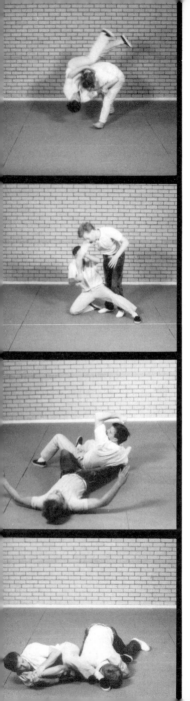

Posture

How you stand determines how well you can respond when attacked. If you are off-balance and falling, you won't be able to make an effective response. Ideally your posture must suit the situation and, since the situation is changing, your posture must too. As your opponent moves, you move with him, maintaining the correct distance at all times. Stance is fluid and free-moving and you cannot afford to be caught on the wrong foot.

At first you may not feel the need to take up an overt defensive posture. Nevertheless take precautions by standing with your feet a natural distance apart and your body turned slightly away from the opponent. If you wish, clasp your hands together in front of your groin. Do not allow the opponent to come too close and step back if he does.

The defensive posture you take up must be capable of rapid change, so your weight must be evenly poised on slightly bent knees. If you straighten your knees suddenly, you can make a fast evasion, advance, or retreat. If you keep your knees straight, this opportunity is lost.

Put one foot in front of the other by about a pace. This is just right to provide

28

freedom of movement. Don't put the leading foot directly in front of the rear one but allow instead a small sidestep. This gives the posture stability and balance. Too little sidestep and your stance loses balance; too much and you expose your groin.

Don't face your opponent square-on. Turn slightly to the side and you will close off a large area of your body from direct attack. Similarly, don't stand directly in front of your opponent. Note where his front foot is and then stand slightly to the closed side of it. This will force him to turn slightly before he can strike at you effectively.

Carry both hands well forward and bring them into the centre-line where they can block and strike effectively (fig. 1). If your left foot leads, then your left

Figure 1

arm must too. Your elbows must be bent so that they can provide the movement for quick punches. Don't over-bend them or your hands will be too close to your own body to block, or too far from your opponent's to punch effectively. Don't straighten your elbows either or you won't be able to snap-punch quickly. Keep your elbows close to your sides, so as not to expose your ribs to direct attack.

Either keep your hands open or roll them into fists. Closed fists look aggressive but prevent your fingers from being grabbed. Open hands are useful for grasping and can close quickly into fists when the need arises.

Distance

It is a good idea to put as much distance as possible between you and an attacker. If possible, run away! Where this is not feasible, then use distance to maximize your effectiveness, whilst minimizing your attacker's.

If your attacker is very tall and you are very short, move in close; that way he cannot use his long reach to advantage. If the attacker is shorter than you are, keep back so he cannot reach you without stepping. If you stand within his effective range, he can punch you in the face with little warning.

Martial art legends abound in unequal competitions between animals. The most popular is between the stork and the bear. In a toe-to-toe situation the stork could not possibly win, but in all the stories the stork kept just out of the bear's range, darting in whenever the opportunity presented itself and inflicting a telling blow.

This is a valid strategy for those who are agile. The trick is not to fall over your own feet as you twist and turn away. I will cover exactly how to move a little later on in this section, so for now let's just say that you must be able to move competently in all directions, so as to maintain optimum distance.

31

Assuming you cannot simply run away, optimum distance is that which allows you the maximum scope for retaliation whilst disadvantaging your attacker. For example, if your attacker throws a punch, you can evade it by furious back-pedalling, opening up a good space between him and you. If you move too far back though, it becomes impossible for you to counterattack without stepping forward yourself and forewarning him.

If you merely evade the attacker without punishing him, he will simply redouble his efforts to corner you. Unless you have the ringcraft of Muhammad Ali, your evasions alone will fail.

Therefore maintain distance so that an attack misses, yet leaves you close enough at hand to deliver a counterattack.

When you train use a mirror that shows the whole of your body. First practise rearward evasion by stepping back a pace. Move quickly and smoothly, keeping your arms and head still. Don't be flatfooted but rest your weight on the balls of your feet, using a springy step.

Avoid giving any indication of what you are about to do by leaning your body this way or that. Distance movements all come from bent knees, which are the key elements in your defensive posture. Move directly and without any

32

hesitation, keeping your face and upper body back from harm's way.

Check the distance you step back and adjust it by the length of your backward pace. The object is to make the technique miss by a safe margin only. Do not go too far back. For very short backward movements, don't step back; just transfer your weight by swinging your body back over the rear leg.

If your left foot is in front of the right, practise sideways evasion by stepping to the left with the front foot and twisting your hips clockwise. The sidestep takes you out of the line of an attack and, the more you step, the further out of line you actually move. Twisting your hips turns you to face your attacker even as you are evading him. If you twist them fully, you can turn your body until it is almost parallel to the attacker's.

Instead of a plain sidestep, step diagonally out and forwards, so that you actually move past and to the side of the attack. This is particularly effective.

Step outwards and backwards with the rear right leg and, at the same time, draw back your left leg and turn your hips away from the attack. As the attack concludes, push your left leg back out and turn your hips to the front once more.

Practise stepping quickly forward so as to follow up an opening. Use your rear right leg to push the left forwards for a pace. As the left stops moving,

33

quickly draw up the right leg, maintaining a constant posture length.

Close from a greater distance by stepping in a semicircle. This has the double advantage of confusing the attacker and taking yourself out of the direct line of attack. Bring your right leg up to the front foot, then step diagonally outwards with it. From the attacker's viewpoint, you seem to be dodging, first to the left, then to the right. Extend the scope of this move by first stepping forwards with the leading foot, then bringing up the rear leg. Don't lean forwards as you step.

Practise all these moves first as advances, then as retreats.

When you turn to face a different direction, look first to check it is safe, then swivel on the balls of your feet. The power for the turn comes from the hips, so the upper body is relaxed and able to respond quickly. Once you have positioned your feet in preparation for the turn, keep your shoulders facing the way they are, while you begin rotating your hips. This builds up pressure in the spine which, when released, snaps the upper body round and gives you a fast turn.

Step across with the back leg, keeping the knees bent and the heel of the rear foot raised. When you have positioned it, turn your hips to face the new direction. Step across a little bit for a stable one hundred and eighty degree turn; step across more to turn further.

Turn also using the front foot by sliding it to the side and swivelling your hips. To turn further, step backwards and out with your front foot.

Never turn blind; always look first and carry an effective guard (figs. 2 & 3).

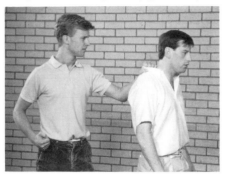

Figure 2

Figure 3

Practise turns together with evasive movements. These are the foundations upon which effective self-defence techniques are built.

When to respond

It is not a good idea to consider a self-defence technique when a knife is being held to your throat. Neither is it sensible to respond to an attack when you are completely incapable of doing so effectively. At such times, you must wait for an opportunity.

For a counterattack to have maximum effectiveness, it must be delivered at precisely the right instant. An identical technique delivered at the wrong time may prove ineffective. Therefore it is important to know when to respond and, conversely, when not to. This is the principle of 'timing'.

Respond when there is a target to aim at – the target being any vital point on the attacker's head or body where the minimum of force produces the maximum of effect. For example, a light strike to the groin will incapacitate more effectively than a hard blow to the shoulder blade. Bide your time until there is a target to aim for.

Time your response so it catches the attacker unguarded and least able to avoid it. When the attacker is squaring up to you, he is poised and ready for action. Even if one or more targets are visible, an attack at this time of maximum preparedness will probably not succeed.

36

If, on the other hand, you time your response so it catches the attacker unawares, it may be more successful.

After the attacker has thrown a powerful punch, he will need a short respite to prepare for the next one. Time your response as his punch finishes, and you stand a better chance of success. Alternatively, those with fast reactions can anticipate the start of an attack and get in first. After all, there is no law that says you must wait for an attacker to strike the first blow.

To effectively utilize these short-lived opportunities, you must remain close to the attacker, relying upon evasion and blocks to protect you during his attack.

Practise timing with a partner. Take up a defensive posture and look at the centre of your partner's chest. As your partner's body weight shifts, respond with evasion and counterattack.

Some teachers recommend looking into the opponent's eyes and speak of the eye-narrowing reflex that precedes a strong attack. I understand and respect this suggestion, but it is my experience that looking into the eyes of a ferocious attacker can sap the will to fight back.

37

Applying force

Force is generated by the muscles of the body. The stronger the muscles, the greater the force generated. Limb movement also occurs through muscle action and the faster that limb travels, the greater energy it develops. The absence of a powerful musculature can be compensated for by using the principles of leverage and by making limb movements faster.

Impact force accelerates a strike or kick until it has sufficient speed and therefore energy to cause the desired effect on impact. Leverage force is gradually exerted on limbs or joints causing pain levels to increase until they are unsupportable and the attack is terminated. Leverage force is also used to unbalance the attacker.

Striking techniques

Jiu jitsu, the martial art upon which I have based my self-defence system, contains many striking techniques. Historically these have been adapted from different sources, though Chinese Shaolin boxing systems figure heavily. In latter years I have studied with masters of other martial arts and increased the number of impact techniques taught.

The strike is seldom an end in itself. Its purpose is to distract, allowing you either to escape, or to use a second technique. Typically it is aimed at one of the vulnerable areas of the body and is then quickly withdrawn. It should begin as close to the target as possible, since this gives less opportunity for it to be stopped or deflected.

The strike is usually delivered in a fast, relaxed movement. I know there are self-defence systems which favour a strong muscular involvement and produce sledgehammer strikes which are effective wherever they land. In my system, the strikes do not have to be so powerful because they are carefully aimed. This is good news for those of us less physically able.

Don't tense as you deliver your strike, be it punch or kick, or you will slow it down. Use a whiplash-like movement with loose joints and only tense the moment you make contact. If you use a fist, hold it loosely formed and, as the fingers first touch the target, tighten it as much as possible. This sudden spasm of the muscles will make the punch heavier.

Keep your face out of harm's way as you punch and don't lead too much with your shoulder. Always keep one hand back to use as a guard. Make the punch as short as possible and move your body behind it to increase power. Have another strike ready in case the first misses and practise multiple hand strikes against a heavy punch bag.

39

Kicks are more powerful than punches because the leg is a bulkier limb. Kick only where there is a clear target. Standing on one leg is not to be recommended in a close-up self-defence situation, so be careful.

Quickly raise the knee of your kicking leg and point it directly at the target. As it reaches maximum height, lash out with the lower leg. Immediately the kick lands, pull it back sharply and set it down carefully.

The fist

The fist is the most commonly encountered hand weapon (fig. 4). It is far from ideal because the skin covering the knuckles is very thin and cuts easily. A good fist is hard to make. The fingers have to be curled into the palm so that the finger joints are out of the way. Most people's fists have the middle finger joints protruding and this is both painful (for you) and ineffective as a weapon.

Don't roll your thumb into your palm because, with impact, it will painfully sprain. Lock the thumb across the middle parts of your fingers and don't let it poke forwards. Land square on the knuckles. Because of the shape of the closed fist, you won't be able to land on all the knuckles so either select those of the index and middle fingers, or those of the middle, fourth and fifth fingers.

Practise punching a heavy but resilient target to train your wrist. The

40

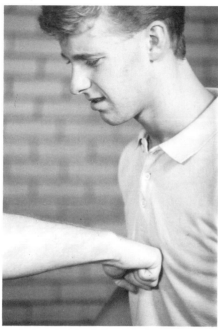

Figure 4

untrained wrist can bend painfully on impact, causing a sprain. Use light practice gloves if you want to save the skin over your knuckles.

Back-fist

There are two other ways to use a fist. You can strike using the upper surfaces of the knuckles as in back-fist, or you can use the rolled edge of the fist under the little finger, as in hammer-fist. When using the latter, land only on the pad of flesh and not on the wrist, or little finger joint.

41

Back-fist is used to attack the sides or front of the face (fig. 5). The elbow is raised until it is pointing at the target and the lower arm is then unrolled out as quickly as possible, so the fist slaps into the target. Keep fist and wrist both relaxed, tightening them as impact is first made.

Figure 5

Palm-heel

Palm-heel is a useful technique for striking to the nose or chin (fig. 6). There is no

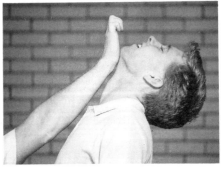

Figure 6

42

chance of the wrist bending and the pad of flesh over the heel of the palm protects the underlying bones from injury.

Curl the hand back and hook the fingers forwards. Fold the thumb across the palm to prevent it snagging in clothing.

Elbow

Elbow strikes are short-range but very powerful. Contact is made with the point of the elbow and not the forearm. To protect the funny bone, make a fist and turn the little finger side to the front. There are three different ways of delivering elbow strikes:

The first is with a swing that uses hips and shoulders to twist the body around. The elbow follows a rising circle into the side of the jaw (fig. 7). The second drops vertically downwards onto the back of the neck (fig. 8). To add weight, bend your knees on first impact. The third method drives the elbow back into the attacker's ribs (fig. 9). Use your hips to

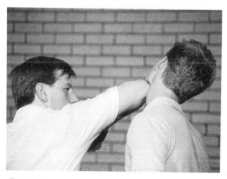

Figure 7

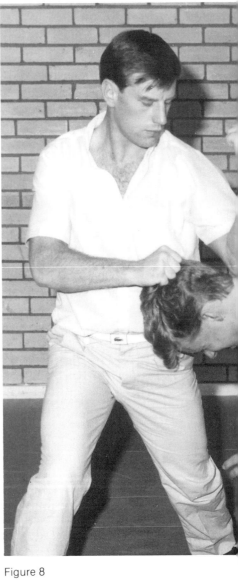

Figure 8

44

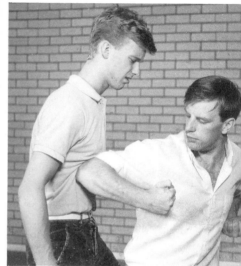

Figure 9

turn behind the strike, giving it more power.

Ball of foot

Kicking with the ball of the foot is quite difficult. Pull your toes back and drop your heel low, so the ball of the foot leads. Keep your toes relaxed so they can move back naturally on impact. At the same time, straighten your instep so it is in line with your lower leg.

Use this to attack the lower stomach and groin (fig. 10).

Instep

Turn your toes downwards and point with your foot. Then strike with the

46

Figure 10

Figure 11

instep, snapping the technique into the groin and returning it quickly (fig. 11). The impact area is just below the ankle.

Heel

Use the heel in three ways. First, use it like a front kick with the ball of the foot pointing into the air. Drive the heel into a target such as the side of the knee (fig. 12). Secondly, use the heel in a stamping action, which drives into the target from a side-on position (fig. 13).

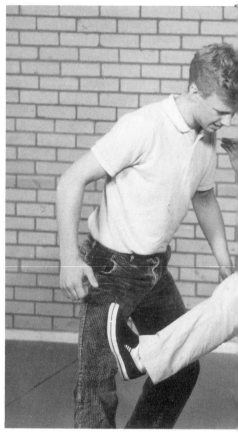

Figure 12

When practising the latter technique, raise your big toe and depress the others to get your foot into the correct position.

Thirdly, from a relaxed position facing the opponent (fig. 14), step across the front of your other foot (fig. 15) and turn your hips suddenly, so your back

48

is towards the opponent (fig. 16). Then drive your heel out sharply into the target (fig. 17).

Practise this whole sequence until it is one continuous, smooth movement.

Whether you are doing a punch or a kick, do not lead with your chin and

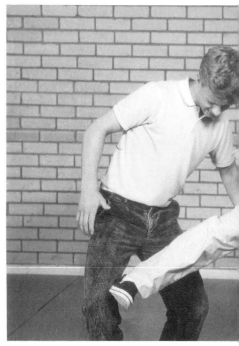

Figure 13

keep a guard at all times.

Leverage

Leverage uses two things: measured force and mechanical efficiency. If I want to lever up a rock, I force a pry-bar under it and then push a strong fulcrum, such as a smaller rock, under the pry-bar. Now when I press down on the end of the bar, the big rock is lifted. This is the principle of leverage.

If I move the fulcrum away from the rock being lifted, mechanical efficiency

50

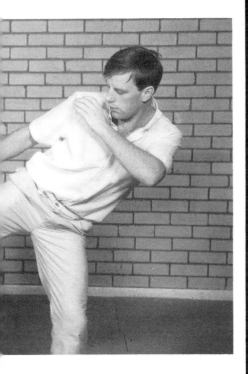

diminishes and I must use more force to accomplish the same task. Leverage uses the length of a limb to apply pressure to a joint.

Consider the following simple system. The defender has seized his opponent's straight arm and twisted it so that the palm faces forwards. The defender's shoulder acts as a fulcrum and, if he pulls down on the attacker's arm, the principle of leverage will raise the attacker onto tiptoes (fig. 18). In this case, the elbow joint is subjected to great

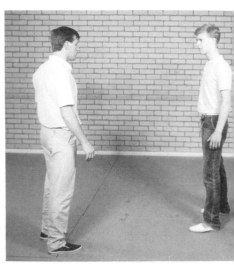

Figure 14

Figure 15

52

Figure 16

Figure 17

pressure and pain is caused. The degree of pain is controlled by downward pressure on the attacker's wrist.

Because pressure is applied at the end of the arm, mechanical efficiency is enhanced and only light pressure is needed to inflict a large amount of pain. If the defender held the opponent's arm closer to the elbow, more effort would be required to cause the same degree of pain. Actually, only one arm is needed to control the attacker (fig. 19).

The bent-elbow lock (fig. 20) applies pressure both to the elbow and the wrist

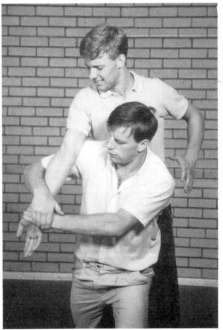

Figure 18

54

joint. The opponent's arm is bent and his forearm forced backwards. The defender's forearm acts as the fulcrum against which his other arm acts, causing the attacker's upper arm to become painfully twisted. The lock is made more efficient by applying pressure to the back of the opponent's hand. This bends the wrist to its limits, producing a second focus of pain.

The above example shows how leverage can be applied both against and with the natural movement of a joint. Considerable pain can be caused by simply

Figure 19

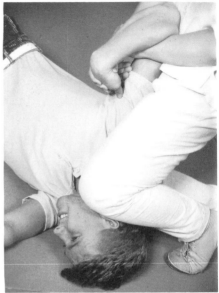

Figure 20

forcing the joint to bend further than it normally would.

If the wrist is over-rotated, the two bones of the lower arm jam against each other. Combining this rotation with a lifting movement brings the would-be attacker to tiptoes (fig. 21).

Leverage has to be applied in your favour, otherwise it is simply a matter of strength versus strength with the stronger person winning. Leverage is most effective against weak joints.

A thumb lock attacks the extended thumb (fig. 22). Catch the thumb between your index and middle fingers (fig. 23) and close your hand into a fist.

Figure 21

Rotate your fist and force the thumb backwards whilst overbending the thumb knuckle (fig. 24). Pushing back the thumb requires two hands (fig. 25) but is otherwise equally effective.

Leverage also works well against fingers. Catch a finger between your middle and fourth fingers. Use your middle finger as fulcrum and force back the captured digit against it, using the pressure of your thumb (fig. 26). The joints can function as their own fulcrums and, forcing the fingers apart (fig. 27), can cause severe injury with little effort.

The following complete sequence

Figure 22

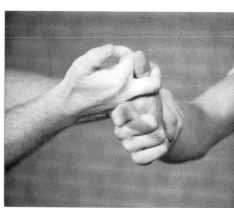

Figure 23

shows the usage of both kinds of force in self defence. Your opponent grabs you in a double lapel hold to which you respond by swinging your left arm up and over his arms. Strike down on them with a circular motion and at the same time pull your right side back, so his

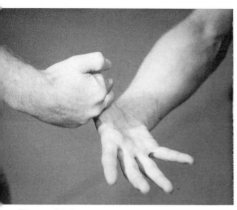

Figure 24

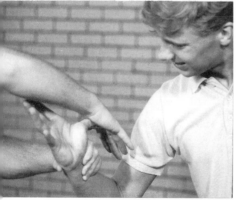

Figure 25

left arm is dislodged. As this happens, reverse your blocking arm and strike with back-fist to the opponent's face. Recover back-fist and seize your opponent's left wrist in an over-hand grasp.

Lean back to take weight off your

Figure 26

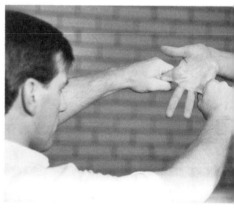

Figure 27

front foot and use it to snap kick into his groin. Lift and move the opponent's trapped left hand in a large circle that keeps his elbow straight. As his arm is brought by your face, strike with palm-heel just above the back of his elbow. Turn your hips and use leverage to force

60

the arm down and close to your body. As you are doing this, fold the opponent's wrist and press on it to subdue him (see sequence A).

Apply effective leverage against the weaker joints of the body

Vulnerable points

There is an ancient Chinese martial art called dim-mok which relies upon knowledge of the body's vital points. Those who study it learn how to cause specific conditions by merely striking certain parts of the body. The theory is that energy flows along certain pathways at certain times and, by disrupting this flow of energy, illness or death can result.

Whilst these theories may or may not be valid, there certainly do exist areas of the body where even superficial pressure or impact can cause dramatic results. The testicles are a well known vulnerable target in the male. There are many others and no study of self defence is complete without reviewing some of the better known.

Use of such vulnerable points makes for a highly effective self-defence system, which may be used unobtrusively to control a would-be attacker. It is best to use them during a grappling situation from which you want to extricate yourself.

The first is to be found deep between the band of muscle which runs along the top of the collarbone. Pressure on the posterior omo-hyoid compresses the brachial plexus, the latter being a network of nerves affecting the arms. The plexus is attacked with the fingers, the thumbs pressing against the opposite side of the muscle (fig. 28). This is a good technique to use when pulling an attacker off his victim.

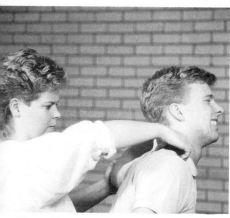

Figure 28

The second pressure point lies in the centre line of the neck, just above the heads of the collarbones. Pushing in here with a finger and curling downwards between the sternocleido-mastoids and the sternothyroid muscles (fig. 29) causes severe discomfort by compressing the nerves of the cervical plexus. This can be used when you are prevented from running away by the attacker grasping your upper arm.

The third point lies just below the ear and behind the edge of the jawbone (fig. 30). Force applied here compresses the

Figure 29

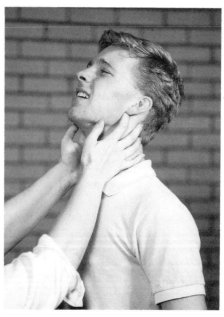

Figure 30

64

temporofacial nerve, causing a severe neuralgia-like pain. Use this when you are caught in a bear-hug that leaves your arms free.

The fourth point is the same complex of nerves, but this time located just below the cheekbones (fig. 31). The index fingers attack the vulnerable points whilst the other fingers anchor the hand to the lower face.

The fifth is particularly useful when you are caught in a side headlock. Reach down the inside of the attacker's thigh and pinch up a fold of flesh between your index finger and thumb. This is extemely painful but is even more so if you trap the small sciatic nerve. Similarly if you pinch the flesh on the inside of the upper arm just below the armpit, you may well irritate the median and ulnar nerves, causing great pain.

Figure 31

Blocking techniques

It is not a good idea to rely totally on an evasion technique to avoid an attack. A block is insurance against the evasion failing. A block is a technique which makes a blow or kick ineffective by either preventing it from developing properly, or by deflecting it away from the intended target. A block can be made by using the shoulders, arms, hands and knees.

There are many different kinds of blocks – some have a general application, others are more specialized. Students practising a martial art over many years can afford to learn a large syllabus; those on a self-defence course cannot. Therefore I have narrowed down the number of blocks to be studied in this book to only two.

Before dealing specifically with those two blocks, I want to talk generally about how blocks work. Ideally a block uses little energy because it harmonizes with the attacking technique and redirects it past its target. It does not meet the attack in a direct confrontation in which the stronger person wins but instead makes use of glancing contact and leverage.

This is not the case with all martial arts, and there are several Chinese and

Japanese schools which use the block as a form of offensive technique. These blocks are designed not only to prevent a successful attack, but also to inflict pain on the attacker. Unfortunately to use them properly requires an extensive training and conditioning programme which is clearly outside the scope of this book.

There are also blocks which use both arms to stop a single attack. Using both arms makes the block stronger, but it also means that you can't respond immediately. Therefore in this elementary course, I suggest you use blocks which require only one arm to deflect an attack.

Wherever possible, the attack is blocked at an early stage before it has accelerated to its maximum speed. The defender must therefore block at a distance and not wait until the blow has nearly reached the target. There are schools of martial art which advocate getting in very close to the attacker. These, however, require hair-trigger responses unavailable to the normal student of self defence.

The block must be performed quickly if it is to stop the attack in time. Therefore keep your body relaxed and do not tense your muscles until the instant when the block makes contact. This will give it added weight.

Turning now to the blocks themselves, first practise a rising block

Figure 32

against a descending attack (fig. 32). The fist leads as the arm moves diagonally upwards across and away from the front of the chest. As the forearm rises past the face, it rotates and turns so that the little finger side of the fist is uppermost, causing the blows it intercepts to glance upwards.

The forearm is maintained at a steep angle so that descending blows tend to slide down it. The fist is held well away from the head, so it can block the attack closer to source. The block is more effective if you step into the attack.

The circular block can be practised with both hands, or with one. Start with both arms crossed above your head (fig. 33). Bring them down in a circle, sweeping a wide area in front of the body (fig. 34). Let the arms separate outwards (fig. 35) and upwards (fig. 36). Move your arms quickly and smoothly, without

68

Figure 33

Figure 34

Figure 35

71

Figure 36

Figure 37

72

hunching your shoulders. This block is effective against a wide range of techniques such as the punch (fig. 37), a double-handed grasp (fig. 38), or a kick (fig. 39). The block does not meet attacks full-on but smacks into the side of them, knocking them off course.

Figure 38

Figure 39

Practise this block by standing with both hands on your head whilst a trusted partner aims slow punches and, later, kicks at you. Move your arms in downwards-curling arcs, to brush each attack to the side. As you become more adept, get your partner to attack slightly faster and harder.

The aim of blocking is to deflect rather than confront

Unbalancing techniques

Unbalancing techniques break the attacker's balance by means of pulls and/or trips. As previously stated, if you resist a shove and then suddenly pull the attacker towards you, he will be unbalanced. Conversely, if he is dragging you along and you first dig your heels in hard then suddenly push him, you will achieve the same result.

One of the most skilful unbalancing techniques is the footsweep, which can be used when the attacker is wrestling with you. As he pushes you, take a full step back and pull him towards you. This forces him to take a step forwards to regain stability.

As his foot is about to set down, give it a hard knock to the inside with the sole of your foot. Carry the footsweep through, so his foot is pushed well to the side. Catch his foot at the right point when he is about to settle weight onto it. If you leave it too late, the technique will not work. Time the footsweep with the pull forwards to achieve best results.

The second technique uses a pull to achieve the same result. Have your training partner lunge forward and try to grab or punch at you. As he does so, move diagonally forwards to his blind

Figure 40

side (fig. 40) and take hold of his shoulders. Step back and pull him sharply backwards. Because his posture is not stable in that direction, he will fall back. Step back as he does so, to avoid flailing fists.

The third technique is an alternative to the last one. After you have stepped through to his blind side, reach down quickly and grasp his ankles (fig. 41). Give them a sharp pull and you will pitch the opponent onto his face (fig. 42). Before he has a chance to recover, step up astride him with one foot past his shoulder and the other at his waist. Grab both of his arms and lift them so his shoulder blades press together (fig. 43).

Figure 41

Figure 42

77

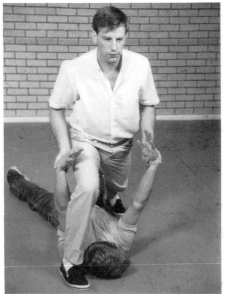

Figure 43

Provided they are kept straight, the degree of leverage used makes it easy to lift the arms even against resistance. Kneel down on your front knee, forcing your heel under his lifted arm. Trap the arm in the angle of your knee as you sit down on it (fig. 44). Then concentrate your attention on the remaining arm, applying a lock to the wrist.

The fourth technique uses a push rather than a pull to unbalance the opponent. Your partner steps forward and grabs you by the throat with both hands. You step back to put pressure on his arms and make a strong circular block that curls over the top of both

Figure 44

arms, jarring them loose from your throat.

Using the same arm, make him lean back with a back-fist to his face. Step forward even as you pull back your fist and hit him in the chest with a double palm-heel. Keep your elbows to your side and make full use of your body weight to knock his weight over the rear leg.

Swing your rear leg through and between his. Hook back strongly into his front foot, striking against the calf muscle. Push him back strongly at the same time, so that he overbalances and falls. If you want to conclude the tech-

nique with an incapacitating attack, kick him in the groin (see sequence B).

This technique is called a reaping throw, because you reap your opponent's leg from under him. Further examples of reaping throws are given in the next chapter.

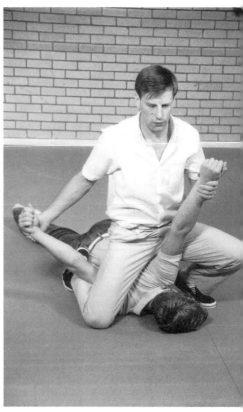

This hold-down locks both arms

Throwing techniques

Tripping and throwing techniques are not in separate categories as they merge into each other. A throw, like a trip, depends upon unbalancing the opponent. This is achieved through leverage force applied after a pre-emptive strike. The strike is necessary because it buys time during which you can set up the throw. The throw uses comparatively complicated movements and must be practised repeatedly until it can be done without conscious thought. It is potentially dangerous to grapple with a stronger person, and only your fast and uninterrupted technique will prevent him winning.

The last section concluded with a description of a simple reaping throw and this one begins with a variant of that technique.

Face your opponent from a range which requires him to step forwards to reach you. For practice purposes, he will attack with a straight kick to your stomach. As he moves, make a sideways evasion to his blind side and bring your right arm down in a circular block which loops under the kicking leg, catches and holds it. Continue the blocking action, lifting the captured leg high.

This will unbalance your opponent and cause him to flail about, so keep a guard near your face. Seize his right

81

shoulder with your left arm and swing your rear leg between his supporting and your left leg. Hook back with your rear leg into his calf and, at the same time, release his foot and swing your right arm hard across his chest.

The opponent's backward lean, combined with the blow on the chest and the hooking away of his supporting leg, will drop him violently onto his back at your feet. As he goes down, keep hold of his right arm, so he can't roll away from you. Follow him down with a punch to his face (see sequence C).

This reaping throw works on both sides and, in the second series, you respond to a kick this time by moving to the opponent's open side. This is more risky because he can hit you with either fist. Deflect his kick as before, with a circling block that curls under and lifts it. Close very quickly until you actually crash into him and grasp the nape of his neck. Keep his trapped leg lifted up and reap the supporting leg, so that he is taken high into the air and dropped, legs open at your feet. Finish with a punch to the groin (see sequence D).

Another group of common throws use the hip to lever an unbalanced opponent up and over. There are many types of hip throw, but the one chosen is particularly effective when there is a wide disparity in size between partners.

Stand a little way back from your opponent so that he has to step to reach you. As he does so and swings a punch, step back and use a circular block. Immediately the punch is deflected, the blocking arm is used again as a back-fist strike to the opponent's face. Do not over-block his punch, or it will take too long to strike back at him.

The back-fist creates an opening during which you seize his punching arm with your left and push upwards into his armpit with the right. Turn your body anti-clockwise into him and bend your knees, so that your centre of gravity is lowered. Continue turning until your backside bumps against his hip.

Slide your right foot back and pull down on his extended and trapped arm whilst pushing up into his armpit. This applies leverage to the elbow joint and encourages him to lift onto tiptoes. Draw his arm forward and down as you bend forward at the waist and this will take him high over your back and forwards onto the mat. Keep hold of his arm and he will land at your feet (see sequence E).

Yet another category of throws involves dropping the body to the floor. The first is known as wheel throw and is best used when your opponent seizes you by the lapels and tries to push you backwards. Hit him across the jaw with a palm-heel that jolts his head back, then quickly step backwards and pull him towards you. Lift your back foot

and kick him in the groin, then fall backwards and draw him up and over you. Keep your leg planted firmly in his groin and hold on to his shoulders as he goes over.

A further throw of this type can be practised as part of a sequence in which your opponent steps forward to punch you in the face. Step back and to the side whilst intercepting the strike with a high circular block that loops over the top of it and then holds on. Keeping the

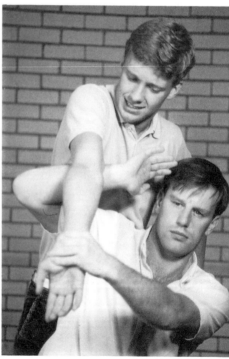

This lock can also be used as an effective throw

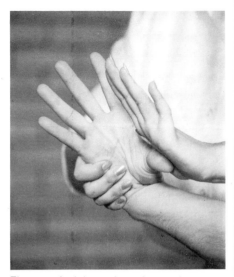

The use of minimum force for maximum effect

arm up, snap kick into the opponent's groin to distract him. Lower the kick across your own front and turn your back on the opponent, dropping down so you finish kneeling on the floor with your back to your opponent. Turn your hips and strike him in the stomach with a back-fist that doubles him forwards and, at the same time, slide your forward knee to the outside of his feet.

All this time you have kept hold of his punching arm, and now you strike upwards with your other arm into his elbow. Draw his wrist forwards, push on his elbow and he will fall over your extended foot. Keep hold of his wrist and he will fall at your feet (see sequence F).

Ground defence

Self-defence situations are seldom neat and tidy, with the parties involved standing a correct distance apart and exchanging elegant textbook techniques. They usually degenerate into a brawl in which one or both parties end up scrabbling around on the ground. Hopefully you will be able to extricate yourself but, in case you can't, some practice in groundwork is useful.

The Marquis of Queensberry Rules do not apply in self defence so, if you get put on the floor, do not expect your opponent to sportingly let you get back up again. If your attacker is still on his feet, the first thing you need is an effective guard. Don't lie on your back, rather turn onto your side and use your feet to spin your body to face attacks from other directions.

Raise your upper leg and bend it across your groin. Bring your lower arm across the front of your face and turn the upper arm down to shield the body. Close your hands into fists so that the fingers can't get damaged in a kicking attack.

You will be unable to launch effective strikes from this position, but at least you will be able to defend yourself against his attacks. You may even be able to trip him, or kick him in the kneecap with the heel of your foot.

If someone does kick at you, don't reach out to block because it won't be strong enough. Keep your arms close to your body and roll into the kick, catching it on the forearm before it has a chance to develop speed and power. Once the kick is smothered, hook your lower arm around and behind the kicking leg, whilst throwing your body's weight against the attacker's legs.

This causes him to topple backwards and he will throw his arms wide to break the fall. Continue rolling over the knees, keeping your arm hooked around the back of the captured leg. If you lean back against the trapped knee, you will put pressure on the joint, causing pain. Without hesitation, slam your elbow into his groin and, if necessary, finish with a back-fist into the solar plexus (see sequence G).

When both of you are on the floor, you can use leverage against the opponent's limbs and/or attacks to his vulnerable points.

If you can keep your wits about you whilst grappling, you can turn any situation to your advantage. Consider the situation where the attacker is kneeling astride and strangling the victim. There is very little time left before the brain starves of oxygen and consciousness is lost, so act decisively. Hit him hard across the side of his jaw with palm-heel

strike. This will momentarily distract him whilst you arch your back, push his shoulder and open up a little distance through which to bring up your knee. Put the sole of your foot against his knee and push hard, causing him to collapse across you. Don't put your foot against his hip or he will fold onto it and jam the technique.

As you are doing this, take his right wrist in your right hand and swing your left leg over the top of his extended right arm. Pressing down on the elbow with your knee will inflict considerable pain. Continue rolling to a kneeling position with your left heel under his throat and your right digging into his solar plexus. Continue pulling on his right arm and bend the wrist down (see sequence H).

Take care when practising this technique with a partner. With you sitting

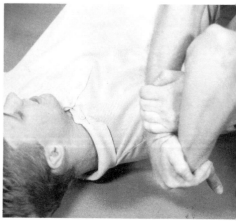

An effective ground-work hold

on his back and your heel in his throat, he can quickly choke. If this begins to happen, he should signal by slapping or kicking the mat to attract attention.

Release immediately your opponent gives in

Escape techniques

As I mentioned previously, attacking the opponent's vulnerable points is a good way to break out of a hold. There are other ways and I have covered some of them in this section.

If the attacker gets hold of you, act quickly to avoid being injured. The longer you leave it, the more he will consolidate his grip and the greater problem you will have escaping from it.

Consider first the situation where the attacker has managed to grab you by the back of your collar and has folded your right hand up behind you in a back hammer. This is a painful hold and a strong attacker can use it to inflict injury. Step forwards on your right leg and simultaneously strike back into the attacker's groin or stomach with a left hammer-fist (fig. 45). Don't pull your fist back after you strike, use it as guard

A low-key escape

against a knee kick.

The hammer-fist creates a distraction which you must use to seize the attacker's right hand with yours whilst you step through in an anticlockwise direction under his arm (fig. 46). Straighten up and fold his right hand into a back-hammer, locking it with your left arm (fig. 47). Stand on his right foot with yours and simply sit back, toppling him over you (fig. 48). Keep hold of his right arm as he goes and roll with him, sliding your right leg under his neck and your

Figure 45

left leg over his throat. Maintain your grip on his straight right arm, folding the wrist down and pulling it back towards you (fig. 49).

If both of your wrists are seized from behind, step forward with your left leg and kick back with your right heel into his groin, knee or lower stomach (fig. 50). Use this distraction to step between his feet whilst raising your left hand high above your head. This twists his wrist and loosens his grasp (fig. 51). Bring your right hand up and seize his left in

Figure 46

an over-hand grasp, which twists it palm towards you and thumb down (fig. 52). Step around with your right leg and at the same time push down on his thumb joint (fig. 53).

If he attempts to punch you with his right hand, release his thumb and block downwards, seizing the wrist and stepping across his body with your right leg (fig. 54). Turn your hips so that your back is towards him and draw his right arm across your stomach (fig. 55). Still keeping hold of both arms, suddenly

Figure 47

94

drop onto one knee and draw him over you. If you keep hold of his extended arms, he will fall at your feet. Whilst he is dazed from the fall, pull his left arm up behind his neck and then kneel on his head with your left leg. Your right leg kneels behind his shoulder blades. Bend his right elbow and wrist into a folding hold (fig. 56).

The third escape is from a single lapel grab. This is almost invariably followed by a punch to the face or a groin kick. Don't bother with the attacker's right

Figure 48

hand – you know exactly where that is and it poses no danger. As soon as your lapel is taken, step back smartly with your right leg and straighten his arm out (fig. 57). As he feels you pulling back, he punches with his left arm. Use your left arm in a downwards circling block, that goes over the top of the lapel hold and stops the punch by knocking it down (fig. 58).

Don't hesitate but immediately back-fist with the blocking arm, catching the

Figure 49

attacker on the side of his face (fig. 59). This distracts him just long enough to allow you to slightly draw back your front foot and snap kick with your instep to the inside of his thigh (fig. 60). As you kick, reach across with your right hand and take his in an over-hand grasp. Press your thumb into the back of his hand, between the thumb and index finger, and rotate his extended arm. Step in close with your left hip and press down on his shoulder with your left hand whilst folding his wrist down

with your right (fig. 61).

Fold his right elbow and lock it into a back hammer with your left arm. Bring your right hand in front of his face and press first upwards against his nostrils and then inwards. This has the effect of straightening him up so he can be marched off (fig. 62).

The fourth escape is from a double-lapel grasp. This time he is likely to attack with a head butt, or knee to the groin. If the former, step back with your right leg and stop his head with a double

Figure 50

98

Figure 51

Figure 52

100

palm-heel (fig. 63). Even as his head connects with your palms, kick him in the lower stomach with your right leg. Leave your right palm on his head and grasp his hair. Grab his right elbow with your left arm and step through with your right leg, hooking back into his right leg while forcing his head back with your right hand, dropping him onto his back in front of you (fig. 64). Keep hold of his right arm and, as he lands, kneel quickly behind him so his extended arm is forced against the joint over your left knee (fig. 65). Finish with a punch to his face or body.

Figure 53

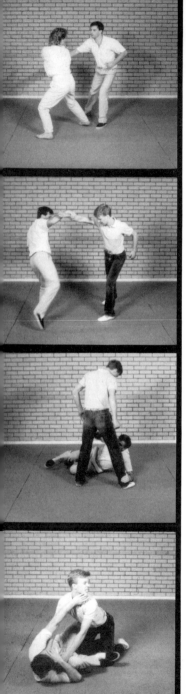

Figure 54

Figure 55

Figure 56

Figure 57

103

Figure 58

104

105

Figure 59

106

Figure 60

109

Figure 61

110

Figure 62

111

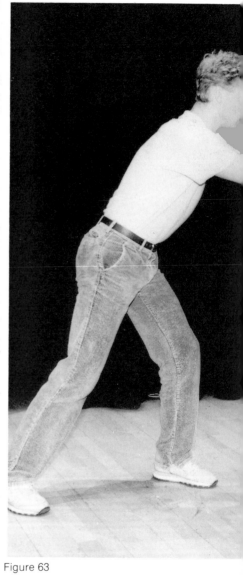

Figure 63

112

113

Figure 64

114

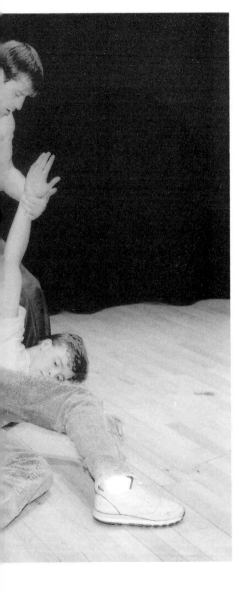

115

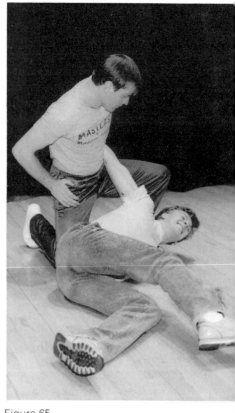

Figure 65

116

Advanced self defence

There is no space in this book to do other than refer generally to some of the more serious attack situations which can arise. These can only be properly dealt with by a competent person, so if you have found the training to your liking, please follow it up with a visit to an approved club. There you will find the necessary equipment and skilled partners to advance your training.

Advanced training provides you with a wider repertoire of techniques to draw from. Additional blocks, strikes, locks and throws supplement a vastly increased groundwork syllabus, which not only allows you to escape but also provides a means of detaining the attacker until help arrives.

On the street you may be faced with more than one attacker. Surprisingly, it is not twice as difficult to deal with two people as it is with one because, unless the two have trained and rehearsed together, they are likely to get in each other's way.

In a two-onto-one situation, distance, timing and speed become even more critical. One response is to feint at one attacker, then strike the other in a vulnerable point. This will give you a little time to deal with the remaining attacker

117

Kicks are both simple to use and effective

119

on a one-to-one basis. If you throw or trip one, make sure he falls in front of the other, obliging the latter to step around him.

If an attacker is armed with a knife, use distance and evasion to stay out of his reach. He will try to grab you with his free hand and pull you onto the knife, so keep back at all times. If you have time, wrap a jacket around your arm and use it to fend the knife off. Alternatively, slip your shoe off and put it over your hand.

If the attacker is using a club, move in close to take away his advantage. A club is not effective at very close distances. Alternatively, keep out of range and retaliate immediately after a swing has missed. Use the same tactics for dealing with attackers wielding iron bars or longer clubs. These lose time shedding momentum after a swing, so use timing to choose the correct moment to respond.

Further training

Few clubs teach pure self defence as such. Most teach self-defence courses together with traditional martial arts training. The only nationally accepted and integrated short self-defence course recognized by the Martial Arts Commission and the British Jiu Jitsu Association is the 'MAC One' course. This consists of fifteen to nineteen lessons and teaches up to an elementary level. It is a good system and one which is easy to learn. Its techniques are taken from a variety of martial arts.

The British Jiu Jitsu Association is currently working with the Martial Arts Commission to develop a more advanced self-defence system which will be called 'MAC Two'. Whereas the MAC One course qualifies the student to the equivalent of a yellow belt in traditional martial art, the MAC Two will qualify him to at least green belt stage. This course is not yet available so, during the interim, those seeking further self-defence training must enrol at a martial arts club.

Most martial arts clubs teach systems which have a self-defence value. The mere act of regularly training with someone rehearses you in the techniques to use, and within a year or two the most

complicated techniques can be performed very quickly and without conscious thought.

Some martial arts have a sporting side to them and, whilst this may not be good in itself for self-defence purposes, dealing with random attacks is very useful for improving anticipation and reaction speed. Some martial arts, such as jiu jitsu, are self-defence orientated and these simulate a true self-defence situation with very powerful random attacks to which the student must effectively respond.

This form of free practice is essential if realism is to be preserved. Constantly repeating an attack/defence combination which permits no variation trains you to apply set techniques, but does not equip you to deal with a spontaneous attack.

The other benefit to training in a self-defence club is that you learn to cope with bumps and bruises. You become aware of the sheer force of an attack and what can go wrong if you don't respond in the right way. A non-co-operative attacker will soon highlight areas where your technique needs improvement.

To help you assess your future training needs, I have included some details of other martial arts practised in Britain. Details of where they may be contacted may be obtained through the Martial Arts Commission.

Aikido

Aikido and jiu jitsu are related. Morihei Ueshiba, the founder of aikido, was a student of a branch of jiu jitsu known as daito ryu aiki-jiu jitsu. This was taught by Master Sokaku Takeda, the latter being related to General Shinra Saburo Yoshimitsu, who is believed to be the founder of daito ryu. Ueshiba became recognized as a teacher grade in aiki-jiu jitsu and developed his own form of it which he named aikido. 'The Way of the Harmonizing of Body and Spirit'.

At first the techniques of aikido were similar to those of jiu jitsu, but Ueshiba's principles of harmony led him to abandon many of the more aggressive techniques in favour of a reactive system that relied totally upon using the attacker's own power against him. In the later developments of aikido, locks against the action of the joint were dropped from practice and the distracting strikes diminished in effectiveness.

Earlier students rebelled against this change. Amongst these were Kenji Tomiki and Gozo Shioda. Tomiki felt that a person's ability in aikido should be tested by free sparring. He developed a sporting system which sharpened the responses of students and caused them to develop techniques suitable to the practice. He also developed two-onto-one competitions and pitted an aikido practitioner armed with a rubber dagger against an unarmed opponent. These

practice forms are excellent for people wishing to learn self defence.

Gozo Shioda would not become involved in sport and maintained his practice at a practical level. He tested his techniques by having opponents attack him with any technique. This is a very good method for training in self defence.

Jiu Jitsu

Jiu jitsu, the 'Compliant Way', had no single point of origin. It formed part of the Japanese warrior's martial art syllabus and was known by various names during its long history. Some of the grappling techniques were taken from the old Chinese systems of chin na, the 'art of seizing'. Striking techniques came from various schools of chuan fa or Chinese boxing (called kempo in Japanese). The latter techniques were not greatly used because of the armour worn, but they came to be important when jiu jitsu's practice spread more widely into the general population.

Jiu jitsu was always related to swordsmanship and its practitioners have long been aware of the importance of timing and distance. Jiu jitsu has always had self-defence connotations though one of its styles became the sport of judo.

Hapkido

Hapkido is the Korean form of aikido. When the Japanese overran the Korean peninsula, they suppressed the tra-

124

ditional Korean martial arts and later replaced them with Japanese ones. Hapkido is one such example. The Hapkido system has all the self-defence advantages of aikido plus strong kicks and punches.

Shorinji Kempo

Shorinji kempo claims to be a form of Chinese boxing based upon that practised in the Shaolin Temple. Its founder, Doshin So, was a student of daito ryu aiki-jiu jitsu and jiu jitsu techniques are in the syllabus. Like hapkido, shorinji kempo uses kicks and punches to vulnerable areas of the head and body.

Free sparring is included in the syllabus, and shorinji kempo is without doubt an effective self-defence system.

Chinese Martial Arts

The Chinese martial arts are popularly known as kung fu. They encompass a great range of systems, both armed and unarmed. The unarmed systems are mainly impact based and are known as 'Chinese boxing'. Some schools of boxing use a lot of strength, speed and power. These are the 'external' schools. 'Internal' schools of boxing use little apparent power, relying instead upon what they term 'inner power'. There are two major types of external boxing, based upon an arbitrary division of China into North and South.

Northern schools favour kicks and

Sequence E
Defence against Punch (1)

Sequence F
Defence against Punch (2)

Sequence G
Rolling Leg Trap

Sequence H
Escape from Prone
Strangle

large movements. Southern schools use more hand techniques and less mobile stances. Some fist-emphasized systems use short-range techniques only, whilst others favour long-ranging punches. These are known as 'short hand' and 'long hand' boxing respectively.

Chinese boxing is not sports orientated – it is a fighting system of great ingenuity. Some systems are so designed that they can be learned completely in only five years whilst others take a lifetime to master. All are worthwhile systems of self defence.

Karate

Karate is the 'Way of the Empty Hand', a fighting system developed in Okinawa. Karate is heavily influenced by Southern Shaolin kung fu and originally used a great many disguised weapons during practice. When the system was introduced to the Japanese mainland, it underwent a change to make it suitable for teaching to large classes.

The Okinawan credited with introducing karate to Japan was Gichin Funakoshi. He met Jigoro Kano, the founder of judo, and was influenced by his teaching. Funakoshi's senior student, Hironori Ohtsuka, was a teacher of jiu jitsu before he took up karate, and many techniques of his earlier art are to be seen in the karate style he founded.

Karate is a very popular martial art with significant self-defence value.

126

Useful contacts

If you enjoyed this book and would like to do some additional training in self defence, then contact any of the following names and addresses – but be sure to enclose a stamped, self-addressed envelope with your enquiry. The first two have computer listings of the nationwide network of approved self-defence clubs, and no matter where you live they will be able to provide the address of your nearest club. The other addresses are local contacts who can direct you to a club within that area.

Robert Clark,
WJJF,
Barlows Lane,
Fazakerley,
Liverpool L9 9EH

Tel: 051 523 9611 (for all national enquiries)

The Martial Arts Commission,
1st Floor Broadway House,
15–16 Deptford Broadway,
London SE8 4PE

Tel: 01 691 3433 (for all national enquiries)

Robert Ross,
40 Crail Place,
Barnehill,
Dundee, Scotland

Terry Parker,
6 Wash Rd.,
Hutton,
Brentwood, Essex

Alan Jenkinson,
29 Ringstead Cres.,
Crosspool, Sheffield 10

Davina Hawkins,
44 Homestead Drive,
Wigton, Leicestershire

Tom Starling,
21 Lakeside Rise,
Blundeston,
nr Lowestoft, Norfolk

Mark Noble,
25, Cloverhill Park,
Belmont,
Belfast, Northern Ireland

John Greenhalgh,
16 Talbot Ave.,
Little Lever,
Bolton, Lancashire

Philip Trueman,
36 Thames Close,
Grangeland Park,
Congleton, Cheshire